Crabapples

Penguins

Bobbie Kalman

Crabtree Publishing Company

Crabapples

created by Bobbie Kalman

For Christina Doyle

Editor-in-Chief
Bobbie Kalman

Writing team
Bobbie Kalman
Niki Walker

Managing editor
Lynda Hale

Editors
Tammy Everts
Petrina Gentile
Greg Nickles

Computer design
Lynda Hale

Color separations and film
Dot 'n Line Image Inc.

Illustrations
Barb Bedell: page 14
Jeannette McNaughton-Julich: pages 8-9, back cover
John Morgan: page 21

Photographs
Frank S. Balthis: page 19 (top)
Wolfgang Kaehler: pages 4, 5, 6 (bottom left), 7 (bottom left),
    10, 12 (top), 13, 14, 15, 19 (bottom), 20, 21, 22-23, 24 (top),
    26 (both), 27 (left), 28, 29, 30 (both)
Joel Simon/Joel Simon Images: title page, pages 7 (top right), 25
Art Wolfe/Art Wolfe Inc.: cover, pages 6 (top left, bottom right),
    7 (bottom right), 11, 12 (bottom), 16-17, 18, 27 (right)
Anna Zuckerman/Tom Stack & Associates: page 24 (bottom)

Printer
Worzalla Publishing Company

Crabtree Publishing Company

350 Fifth Avenue   360 York Road, RR 4,   73 Lime Walk
Suite 3308   Niagara-on-the-Lake,   Headington
New York   Ontario, Canada   Oxford OX3 7AD
N.Y. 10118   L0S 1J0   United Kingdom

Cataloging in Publication Data
Kalman, Bobbie, 1947-
    Penguins

(Crabapples)
Includes index.

ISBN 0-86505-624-2 (library bound)   ISBN 0-86505-724-9(pbk.)
This book looks at penguin homes, babies, appearance and
behavior. It shows 18 types of penguins.

1. Penguins - Juvenile literature. I. Title. II. Series: Kalman,
Bobbie, 1947-   . Crabapples.

QL 696.S473K35 1995   j598.44'1   LC 95-24624
                                              CIP

What is in this book?

What are penguins?	5
Many penguins	6
The penguin family tree	8
A penguin's body	10
Penguin homes	12
Hunters and hunted	14
In the water	16
Moving on land	18
Staying warm, keeping cool	20
Rookeries	23
Mating	24
Baby penguins	26
Growing up	28
Penguin facts	30
Words to know & Index	31
What is in the picture?	32

What are penguins?

Penguins may not look like other birds, but they are birds. Like all birds, penguins are covered with feathers. They are **warm-blooded**, which means their body stays the same temperature no matter how warm or cold their surroundings are. All birds, including penguins, hatch from eggs.

Many penguins

Penguins have different shapes and colors. Some penguins have only black and white feathers. Others, such as the emperor penguin on the left, have brightly colored patches of feathers. Special head markings help penguins recognize other members of their species.

The most common penguins, adélies, are only black and white.

Yellow-eyed penguins are the only penguins with a golden "crown."

Some penguins, such as this rockhopper, have long crests of feathers on top of their head. Some crests are yellow, and others are orange.

Penguins also differ in size. The largest is the emperor penguin, which is about 120 centimeters (four feet) tall. The smallest is the little blue penguin. It is the size of a duck.

Magellanic penguins have black and white stripes on their chest.

Little blue penguins have feathers that look more blue than black.

The penguin family tree

There are eighteen types of penguins. Scientists have divided these penguins into six groups. Some penguins look similar. Can you see the differences?

Scientists believe that the penguin's closest living relatives are sea birds such as the albatross and shearwater.

albatross

shearwater

emperor   king

yellow-eyed

Crested penguins

macaroni

erect-crested

rockhopper

Fiordland

royal

Snares

Brushtail penguins

chinstrap

adélie

gentoo

Fairy penguins

little blue

white-flippered

Banded penguins

Galapagos

black-footed

Magellanic

Humboldt

A penguin's body

Penguins have a very poor sense of smell.

Scientists think that penguins can see better underwater than they can on land.

A penguin's smooth, **streamlined** body helps it travel quickly through the water.

Most birds have hollow bones to help them fly, but a penguin has solid bones that allow it to dive into water.

A penguin uses its razor-sharp beak to fight off enemies.

A penguin has fleshy spikes on its tongue and inside its mouth to help it hold onto its slippery food.

Millions of years ago, a penguin's flippers were wings, but now they are shaped like paddles for swimming.

A penguin has a **preen gland** near its tail. The preen gland makes the oil that the penguin uses to waterproof its feathers. After each swim, the penguin **preens**. It uses its beak to arrange its feathers and spread oil through them.

A penguin's feathers are short and stiff. Once a year, old feathers fall out as new ones grow. This change is called **molting**. It takes several weeks for a penguin to molt.

Penguin homes

Penguins live on the coasts of Antarctica, South Africa, New Zealand, Australia, Chile, Peru, and the Galapagos Islands. All these places are south of the equator.

Penguin homes, or **habitats**, differ. Some are cool places where trees and plants grow. Others are warm, dry areas. Many penguins live in Antarctica, where the land is always covered in ice and snow. Penguins do not live in the Arctic!

Penguins spend more than half their lives in the oceans around their habitats. They enjoy swimming in these oceans because the water is always cool or cold.

Hunters and hunted

Penguins are **carnivores**. They eat animals such as squid, fish, and krill. They dive for their prey and grab it with their sharp beaks.

A penguin's mouth, throat, and stomach stretch, allowing it to swallow its prey whole. A penguin can swallow prey that is almost as big as itself!

Penguins are hunters, but they are also hunted by other animals. Birds such as skuas, sheathbills, and gulls snatch penguin eggs and babies from their nests. These birds also kill weak or old penguins.

An adult penguin's enemies include orcas, sea lions, and leopard seals. Leopard seals are such good hunters that penguins will not go into the water if they see one nearby.

In the water

Penguins cannot fly, but they do flap their flippers underwater as other birds flap their wings in the air. As they swim, penguins steer with their feet and tail. Penguins can swim very quickly.

When penguins swim long distances, they shoot out of the water, take in air, and dive under again. This leaping is called **porpoising**.

Penguins are able to hold their breath underwater for a long time. Emperor penguins can hold their breath for up to twenty minutes!

A penguin's black-and-white coloring is called **countershading**. Countershading helps **camouflage** penguins in the water. An enemy swimming beneath a penguin cannot see its white belly against the bright sky above. An enemy swimming above a penguin cannot see its black back against the dark water below.

Moving on land

Because their bodies are designed for swimming, most penguins find walking difficult. To keep their balance as they waddle, penguins must lean forward and hold out their flippers.

Many penguins, such as the rockhopper, find it easier to hop from rock to rock than to waddle.

Some penguins, however, can move quickly on land. On soft snow, an adélie penguin can outrun a person!

When penguins get tired of walking, they **toboggan**. They flop onto their belly and push themselves along with their flippers.

Staying warm, keeping cool

It is not good for penguins to be too hot or too cold, so these birds have ways to control their body temperature.

All penguins have a thick layer of fat, called **blubber**, under their skin. Blubber helps keep penguins warm because their body heat cannot escape through their thick fat.

A penguin's feathers also keep it warm. The outer feathers are waterproof to keep cold water away from the skin. Fluffy feathers, or **down**, trap warm air between a penguin's skin and its waterproof feathers.

When penguins feel too hot, they ruffle their feathers or hold out their flippers to let warm air escape.

Baby penguins cannot fluff out their thick feathers. They flop down on their belly and stretch out their feet behind them. They release heat through the soles of their feet!

Rookeries

Penguins nest in large groups called **rookeries**. Most penguins spend the year hunting far away from their rookery. They return to the rookery once a year to have babies.

Some rookeries are on the shore. Others are inland. Some are on bare ice. Others are in forests and caves. In warm areas, rookeries are often underground!

Rookeries range in size from a few penguins to more than a million! They are often crowded and noisy. You can smell a rookery from far away because of the **guano**, or droppings.

Despite their huge populations, most rookeries are orderly. Penguins leave small roadways between their nests and try not to disturb their neighbors, who might nip them if they get too close.

Mating

Penguins usually choose the same partner, or **mate**, every year. The male reaches the nest site first and waits for the female to join him. Penguin couples are very excited to see one another again.

A male without a mate points his beak straight up, flaps his flippers, and squawks loudly. He hopes that his **ecstatic display** will attract a female.

When a single male tries to steal another penguin's mate, his attempt can lead to trouble! The two males stretch as tall as they can, puff out their chest, and try to bully each other in a **bluffing** contest. One usually runs away before he is hurt.

Baby penguins

Penguin babies are called **chicks** or **hatchlings**. Most female penguins have one or two chicks each year.

The parents take turns **brooding** their egg. They guard the egg and keep it warm. Several weeks later, the chick hatches.

The chick breaks a small hole with its **egg tooth**—a small, sharp bump on the tip of its beak. The egg tooth will fall off after a few days.

26

Penguins are good parents. Both mother and father penguins look after their eggs and chicks. Parents care for their babies until they are able to hunt for themselves. They also protect the chicks from enemies and harsh weather.

The chick cracks the egg around the middle and pushes the halves apart with its feet. It takes up to two days to get out of the egg!

The chick pecks at the bottom of its parent's beak to say "feed me." The parent then brings up, or **regurgitates**, food for the chick.

Growing up

A penguin chick grows quickly. Soon both of its parents have to hunt in order to feed it. While its parents are away, the chick huddles with other chicks for warmth and protection.

A group of chicks is called a **crèche**. Crèches are guarded by adults that do not have chicks of their own. These guardians are called **aunties**.

Several weeks after it is born, the chick loses its baby down, and its adult feathers start to show. Losing down is called **fledging**. Some scientists think fledging makes chicks grumpy.

Penguin facts

 Penguins often follow one another in a line. It looks as if they are playing a game of "follow the leader."

Penguins is able to find and recognize its mate and chick by their unique voices.

Sometimes penguin mates cannot get along. When this happens, they "divorce" one another and look for new mates.

Emperor penguins have a flap of skin, called a **broodpouch**, near their belly. They rest the egg on their feet and cover it with their broodpouch to keep it warm.

Penguins gesture to one another in many ways. They bow, roll their eyes, and fluff up the feathers on top of their head. Scientists are not sure what these gestures mean.

Words to know

blubber A thick layer of fat under an animal's skin

brood To sit on eggs so they will stay warm and hatch

camouflage Patterns or colors that help an animal blend into its environment

carnivore An animal that only eats other animals

countershading Dark-and-light coloring that camouflages an animal as it swims

crèche A group of penguin chicks

ecstatic display A male penguin's movements to attract a mate

fledging The condition of a baby bird when it loses its down

guano Bird droppings

krill Tiny sea creatures that look like shrimp

molt To lose old feathers and grow new ones

porpoising The act of leaping from water and diving back in

preening The action of a bird cleaning its feathers with its beak

Index

adélie penguin 6, 9, 19
babies 15, 21, 23, 26-27, 28, 29, 30
beak 10, 11, 14
blubber 20
camouflage 17
eggs 5, 15, 26, 27, 30
emperor penguin 6, 7, 8, 17, 30

feathers 5, 6, 7, 11, 21, 29, 30
flippers 10, 16, 18, 19, 21, 24
food 8, 10, 14, 27, 28
habitats 12-13
little blue penguin 7, 9
Magellanic penguin 7, 9
mating 24-25, 30

penguin family tree 8-9
predators 15, 17
rockhopper penguin 7, 9, 18
rookery 23
swimming 8, 10, 11, 12, 16-17, 18
walking 18-19
yellow-eyed penguin 6, 8

What is in the picture?

Here is more information about the photographs in this book.

page:	
cover	A mother and baby penguin
title page	King penguins are very curious.
4	A crèche of emperor chicks
5	Gentoo penguins live at sea for three to five months each year.
6 (top)	Emperor penguins can weigh 40 kilograms (90 pounds).
6 (bottom right)	Adélie penguins build nests by piling pebbles with their beak.
6 (bottom left)	Scientists think that there are only 5,000 yellow-eyed penguins.
7 (top)	Rockhoppers are the most aggressive penguins.
7 (bottom right)	Little blue penguins live in Australia and New Zealand.
7 (bottom left)	Magellanic penguins have a call like that of a braying donkey.
10	King penguins are almost as large as emperor penguins.
11	Macaroni penguins hop on two feet, as rockhoppers do.
12 (top)	Emperors live on Antarctica and in the oceans around it.
12 (bottom)	Magellanic penguins nest underground to escape from the sun.
13	Some gentoo penguins live on the Falkland Islands.
14	King penguins can swim faster than most birds can fly.
15	Leopard seals chase penguins on land as well as in the water.
16-17	Adélie penguins swim in freezing cold water.

page:	
18	Rockhoppers have claws on their feet to help them climb.
19 (top)	This gentoo is tobogganing.
19 (bottom)	On land, adélie penguins can outrun leopard seals.
20	Adélie penguins enjoy riding on floating ice blocks.
21	Gentoo penguins used to be called Johnny penguins.
22	King penguins do not travel far from their rookery.
24 (top)	These rockhoppers greet one another with a "mutual" display.
24 (bottom)	Two king penguins are engaged in a bluffing game.
25	Penguin mates, like these king penguins, are very affectionate.
26 (left)	Gentoo penguins brood their eggs for about 33 days.
26 (right)	Chinstrap chicks are ready to hatch after 35 days.
27 (left)	Penguin parents do not help their chicks hatch.
27 (right)	Penguin parents regurgitate food for their chicks.
28	Unlike these emperor penguins, chicks raised in warm areas do not form crèches.
29	King penguin chicks stop fledging at one and a half years.
30 (top)	Kings follow each other to sea.
30 (bottom)	Male emperors brood their egg for six weeks.

2 3 4 5 6 7 8 9 0 Printed in the U.S.A. 4 3 2 1 0 9 8 7 6